Nothing But A Blaze

The Indian War on the Lower Rogue River

by

James Boyle

ISBN 13: 978-1720676133
ISBN 10: 1720676135

Scribe Memnon Press
30327 Driftwood Drive
Gold Beach, OR 97444

Contents

Rogue War Timeline

1856

Feb 22-23   Attack on Gold Beach Guard camp near Tututni village
Attack on B. Wright/John Poland
Attack on Geisel homestead
Attack on Ellensburg
        Survivors flee to Ft. Miner (about 100 people 8 white women, 4 Indian women)
All settlements from Humbug Mountain to the Chetco River burned
        25 to 35 whites killed

Feb 27   Rowboat relief capsizes in surf
Mar 3   Potato foragers killed
Mar 6   Mrs. Geisel and daughters ransomed
Mar 18-19   Militia ambushed at mouth of Pistol R.
Mar 18   Shasta Costa village destroyed by Army

Mar 20	Army arrives at Ellensburg ruins. Skirmish near mouth of Rogue.
Mar 21	Ft. Miner relieved
Mar 25	Gold Beach Guards find Tututni village abandoned; burn it
Mar 26	Mikontunne village attacked and destroyed
Apr 24	Militia ambushes Indians near Lobster Creek.
Apr 29	Chetcos attack pack train coming from Crescent City
May 27	Battle at Big Bend
June 6	Battle at Painted Rock
June 29	Chief John surrenders to Cpt. Ord.
July 2	Ord arrives with prisoners at Ft. Orford
July 8	Tututni shipped out of Ft. Orford
July 9	Remaining Tututnis marched north

1858

June 16	Indian camp near Giesel ruins attacked by militia

Chapter One

A Forgotten Corner of Oregon

The south coast of Oregon, including the lower Rogue River area, has long been a forgotten backwater. Even during the immigration fervor of the 1840's, when thousands of hardy pioneers trekked for months over the Oregon Trail, they weren't heading to the south coast of Oregon. They settled in the Willamette Valley for the most part and along Puget Sound farther north. No one came to the South Coast.

When gold was discovered in California in 1849, some immigrants bypassed Oregon entirely and headed directly to California. Others, already settled in the Oregon Territory, felt the lure of gold fever and established a trail south from the Willamette Valley settlements to the gold fields in the Sacramento Valley. This trail crossed the upper reaches of the Rogue River near the present communities of Medford and Grants Pass. Some of those travelers liked the country on the upper Rogue and began settlements there.

No one consulted the peoples who were already living there, either for permission to cross their lands, or to build communities among them. This led to conflicts.

Still, the South Coast was ignored.

Other than an expedition by explorer and trapper Jedediah Smith in 1828 and the occasional shipwreck, no European or American paid any attention to the South Coast until Capt. William Tichenor decided in 1851 to establish a settlement at a deep-water cove south of Cape Blanco. He dropped nine men off and sailed back to San Francisco for supplies. Unfortunately, the local Quatomah band of Indians objected to this incursion and the Battle of Battle Rock ensued. The Americans, though able to fight off the attack, were forced to sneak away during the night.

So why was this area ignored for so long?

Mostly, it was a matter of terrain. The south coast of Oregon is covered by steep, heavily-forested mountains that begin at the edge of the Pacific and quickly rise to 4000 feet in the interior. Often the mountains march right to the ocean itself in the form of headlands and rocky cliffs falling directly into the pounding surf. Cutting through these mountains are fast, cold rivers like the Rogue, Pistol, and Chetco. These rivers cut steep, narrow valleys between the mountains with more rapids than eddies. Perhaps as important as any feature is the fact that the rivers of the south coast tend to form sand bars across their mouths that prevent large ships from entering and make crossing those bars dangerous even for smaller craft.

So, the South Coast was a country one couldn't reach easily. The mountains were nearly impassable. Even today, there are no roads directly linking the communities of Curry County with the interior valleys. Travelers have to drive south to Crescent City, California before heading northeast around the mountains toward Grants Pass and Medford, or north to Bandon, in Coos County, and then east toward Roseburg. The town of Gold Beach didn't even have a wagon road to Port Orford until 1890. Coupled with the difficulty the river bars present to shipping by sea, the terrain made supplying a colony of settlers extremely challenging.

Another feature of the terrain was even more responsible for the late development of the South Coast: the lack of arable farmland. Because of the steepness of the mountains and the narrowness of the river valleys, the South Coast does not have a great deal of land suitable for farming. In the middle of the 19th Century, the United States was still largely an agricultural country. Most of the immigrants traveling over the Oregon Trail were looking to secure a land claim and farm that land. There simply wasn't enough of it on the South Coast to draw them. Farm land was much better and easier to work in the Willamette Valley, Western Washington, or even the highlands of the upper Rogue and Umpqua basins.

In short, there were very few reasons a pioneer family would want to homestead on the South Coast and many reasons to go somewhere else.

Perfectly happy with this situation were the Athabascan-speaking peoples who lived on the South Coast and had lived here for thousands of years. American histories call them Tututni, though that was actually just the name of one of the larger villages on the Rogue. They lived in small communities throughout the area: the mouths of Floras Creek and the Sixes River north of Port Orford; near the town of Port Orford itself; the mouths of Mussel and Euchre Creeks, between Port Orford and Gold Beach; the mouth of the Rogue River and several places along the river itself; the mouth of Pistol River and near Whaleshead Creek, between Gold Beach and Brookings; and the mouth of the Chetco River.

These peoples were not a tribe as most Americans conceive of a tribe: a single political entity, led by a chief. Instead, they were a collection of independent villages that shared similar language and cultures but were politically independent. Their villages were mostly kinship groupings, each led by its own chief. No one had the political title of head chief as an American observer might expect.

The peoples of these villages harvested the plentiful salmon in the rivers; shellfish, seaweed, and the occasional whale from the beach; and deer and elk from the mountains. Women gathered camas bulbs from the river meadows, berries, and acorns from the oak thickets. Travel was over the rivers in dugout canoes fashioned from cedar trunks or, less often, on foot over trails linking the villages through the mountains. Their dwellings were partially dug into the river bottoms, with walls and roofs fashioned from split cedar planks. Their houses also held their stores of dried salmon to feed them through the winter.

The Indians of the South Coast had suffered from disastrous epidemics like their neighbors, but their isolation had also offered some protection. While the Chinook, Tillamook, and Calapuya of the northern valleys suffered as much as a 95% death rate, the Tututnis only lost about two thirds of their population to pandemic disease.[1]

By the middle of the Nineteenth Century the peoples of the South Coast numbered a little less than two thousand people. And for most of that time they had been left alone to live in relative peace as they had for thousands of years.

Then, in the spring of 1853, gold was found in the black sand deposits on the beach near the mouth of the Coquille River in Coos County. Shortly after, someone noticed that there was a great deal of similar black sand on the beaches near the Rogue River.

There was gold on the south coast of Oregon.

And gold changed everything.

Chapter Two

War and Rumors of War

One of the great dangers of writing history is making assumptions about conditions in any particular place and time, especially when there is little to no documentation. Did the native peoples of the South Coast know of the problems around them? There is no way of knowing for certain, but it stretches the imagination to think they lived in total isolation, completely unaware of the conflicts between the Americans and their Indian neighbors in the lands surrounding them. After all, they traded and intermarried with neighboring tribes, certainly with the peoples living on the upper portion of the Rogue River and with others to the north and south. If they weren't aware of the details (not in the manner that the modern world considers news) they probably heard plenty of stories that would be passed from person to person over meals, trading sessions, and other social gatherings.

As more and more whites began to build cabins and sluice boxes amid the black sand deposits along the coast, the local Tututni villages would almost certainly have heard of the brief war between the Takelma of the upper Rogue and the whites (June 1 to September 8, 1853). That brief war had resulted in those Takelma peoples giving up most of their land in exchange for a shaky peace and a reservation in the Table Rock area on the north bank of the Rogue River. [2]

To the south, they would have heard about the December 1853 attack by militia from Crescent City, California on the Tolowa village of Yontocket, during the gathering for the annual *Nee-dash* "world renewal" religious ceremony. Estimates have the number of Tolowa men, women, and children killed at 450. [3] The Tolowa were also Athabascan-speaking, like the peoples on the South Coast; the two peoples often intermarried. The attack almost certainly would have been a topic of discussion.

Shortly after, on January 28, 1854, a group of forty white miners from the community of Randolph, Oregon (sixty miles north of the Rogue, near present-day Bandon) led by George Abbott staged a dawn attack on the sleeping Nasomah village at the mouth of the Coquille River, killing fifteen men and one woman, and taking the remaining women and children prisoner. Their stated reason for the attack was to preempt an Indian war. [4]

Then on February 15, a group of white miners, led by A.F. Miller, who was outraged that the local Indians were undercutting his ferry rates, attacked and burned the two Chetco villages at the mouth of the Chetco River. Twenty-six men and women were killed, most shot down while trying to flee. Two men who tried to resist with bows and arrows were burned to death in their houses.

At the urging of the Indian Agent Joel Palmer, Miller was arrested, taken to Fort Orford and held six weeks before trial. No Indians were allowed to testify against him and those testifying on his behalf were the same friends who'd participated in the massacre. The Justice of the Peace released Miller, citing: "the ground (sic) of justification and want of evidence to commit." [5]

In none of these incidents was the U.S. Army the force committing the attacks. The American forces were all vigilantes, or militia groups formed from the local population of miners and settlers. Like the vigilance committees of San Francisco and the Montana gold fields, their purpose was supposed to be self-protection. However, just as with the vigilance committees, that's often not how the system really worked in practice.

In 1856, the United States had a standing army of only 16,000 officers and men, not nearly large enough to adequately protect a nation stretching from the Atlantic to the Pacific coasts. To fill this security hole, the States and Territories used a system of local militias to address short-term emergencies. The governor would authorize the activation of the militia and local men would sign up, usually for a six-month enlistment. Though militia volunteers were often paid a monthly stipend, they were expected to provide their own weapons, clothing, and horses. Officers were usually elected by the members, though occasionally an officer would be appointed by the governor as a political favor.

Because of this system the militias were almost always poorly trained, poorly disciplined, and poorly led. With only a six-month enlistment, the members weren't in the militia long enough for any serious training. Officers often had no military experience and, while they were usually popular with the rank and file, were often unable to make them obey orders, even if they knew what orders to issue. (Source)

The system also tended to reinforce any biases within the community at large. In many of the mining communities of northern California and southern Oregon, the miners generally didn't want peace with the neighboring

Indians as much as they wanted the Indians to be gone and weren't particular about how that was achieved. Naturally, a group of men with this opinion elected leadership that shared that view. For example, the militia group formed in Crescent City, California gave themselves the telling nickname: "The Exterminators."[6]

The natives of the South Coast weren't wholly innocent bystanders either. Some settlers were killed, as were isolated miners and the occasional traveler. Property and livestock were also sometimes appropriated. Whether these were simply crimes, instances of retaliation for perceived wrongs, cultural differences, or a combination of all three is unclear.

In December of 1854, the "Exterminators" again attacked a Tolowa village north of Crescent City, this time near Lake Earl. The village of Achulet was burned and somewhere between 65 and 100 men, women, and children killed. Again, the Tolowa had been gathered for their annual *Nee-dash* "world renewal" ceremonies.[7]

Through all this, a tense peace held over the lower Rogue River, largely through the efforts of the Oregon Territorial Indian Agent, Joel Palmer and his sub-agents. One of them, J.L. Parrish conducted a detailed survey of the native communities of the south coast in 1854, which provides an interesting snapshot of their populations at the time.

Village	Men	Women	Boys	Girls	Total
Nasomah	18	20	10	11	59
Choculeatan	30	40	18	17	105
Quatomah	52	45	22	23	142
Cosulthoutun	9	9	6	3	27
Euquachee	24	41	18	19	102
Yahshute	39	45	24	12	120

Tututun	39	47	23	12	121
Mackanotin	32	58	17	17	124
Shistakoostee	53	61	23	16	153
Chetlessnatin	16	15	11	9	51
Wishtenatin	18	26	13	10	67
Cheattee	117	82	23	16	238
Total	**447**	**489**	**208**	**165**	**1309**
Total Rogue	**163**	**211**	**87**	**57**[8]	**518**

The white population was similarly small. Port Orford, the only actual town in the area, was a collection of a couple of dozen houses and a population of a little over a hundred people. Twenty-five soldiers of the U.S. 4th Infantry Regiment were stationed at nearby Fort Orford.[9]

Estimates have between seventy-five and a hundred whites working the mining claims near the mouth of the Rogue River, home to the community known by various names, depending who you talked to. It had been called Sebastapol, Logtown, Prattsville, Ellensburg, and Gold Beach. For simplicity, this history will call it Ellensburg.

For those familiar with the modern town of Gold Beach, it's easy to assume that the modern town is just a more developed version of 1856 Ellensburg. This is not entirely true. The modern town is built on a plateau or shelf well above the river and beach, which protects the inhabitants from most floods. The community of Ellensburg, on the other hand, was built on the south bank of the Rogue River, just about where the modern Post Office and Port offices are located. This facilitated the loading and off-loading of goods and passengers from the small schooners that supplied the community.

Ellensburg, in 1856, consisted of three commercial buildings: the hotel owned by Coburn and Warwick, and two mercantile stores owned by F.H. Pratt and J.W. Upton.

The rest of the community were simple cabins, "shanties," and various sluices and other mining structures.

By far, the majority of the residents of the Ellensburg area were young unmarried men. (Of the hundred or so people, six to ten were women; about 20, children). Most of these men were veterans of the frontier, a rough and tumble bunch, used to living outside the conventions of civilized society. Many of them had come to the South Coast gold fields after failing in those of California. A sizable number were first-generation immigrants to the United States, mostly from Europe, mainly the German states and Ireland.[10]

They were outnumbered by the local natives five-to-one and they knew it.

Into this tense but peaceful situation was thrust another wild card when Joel Palmer appointed Benjamin Wright Indian sub-agent for the South Coast after J. L. Parrish resigned. He was an interesting choice. Benjamin Wright had a well-deserved reputation as an "Indian fighter." He had been a leader of the militia out of Yreka, California during the Modoc war of 1852-3, where he made a good living taking Modoc scalps for the California government.[11]

In November of 1852, Wright secured his fame by inviting a band of Modoc to meet for peace negotiations. During the night, he had his militia troops surround the sleeping Modoc camp and at daybreak, open fire. At least 50 Modocs were killed. Wright and his men scalped the victims and returned to Yreka, which welcomed him as a hero.[12]

There are also reports that a drunken Wright stripped the clothing from Chetco Jenny, the government Tututni interpreter and his mistress at the time and drove her naked down the rain-soaked boardwalk of Port Orford with a riding crop.[13]

Now Benjamin Wright was charged with the difficult job of maintaining peace between the native peoples of the

South Coast and the miners working their claims. By all accounts, he worked hard at this job and did so fairly.

One source (which may be apocryphal) had Wright meeting in Crescent City with the local "Exterminators" militia. He told them they were never, under any circumstances, to cross the border into the Oregon Territory. If they did, he warned them, there would be "fearful consequences." At about the same time, he warned the Indians living along the Chetco River in the southern portion of the area, to "not fight back against the whites...flee into the mountains when they attack you." And never seek vengeance against whites south of the California border because doing so would give the "Exterminators" an excuse to attack them.[14]

In August of 1855, Indian Superintendent Joel Palmer arranged to meet with all the Indians along the Rogue River to negotiate terms of a new treaty. Officials from the military and Oregon Territorial Government were to meet with the Tututni leaders in the shadows of a myrtle grove across the Rogue River from the main Tututni village. The Government's idea was: the only way to protect the native population from conflict with the white miners was for the Tututnis to give up their lands and move away. In exchange, they would receive blankets, metal cooking utensils, foodstuffs, and a new Reservation along the north coast of Oregon, far from any white settlements.

The negotiations almost ended before they began.

A local Tututni man was confronted by a miner named James Buford about riding an allegedly stolen horse. The Indian shot Buford in the upper arm and fled. The wound was described as minor. Buford gathered some friends and found the Indian man in the village on the Pistol River. They were going to hang him right then, but Indian Agent Wright intervened, took custody of the Indian, and turned him over to the Federal troops in the area for the treaty negotiations.

A short time later, the Tututni man in question was in a canoe on the Rogue with a second Indian and some soldiers when another canoe drew alongside. It contained Mr. Buford and two friends named Watt and O'Brien. They fired on the first canoe, killing the suspect Indian immediately. The soldiers returned fire, killing all three miners.[15]

For a while it seemed the incensed miners around the Rogue were going to fight both the Tututnis and the Federal troops. The Tututni fled the treaty grounds. Cooler heads managed to defuse the situation and outright warfare was averted. Eventually, the Tututnis were persuaded to return and agree to the terms of a treaty, which was signed by all parties on September 13, 1855.[16]

It seemed peace had been secured. The Tututnis had agreed to vacate their homelands in exchange for peace and a distant reservation they had never seen. (And which didn't actually exist).

On October 7, 1855, self-proclaimed "Major" James Lupton, from Yreka, California, came to Jacksonville, Oregon (about 130 miles up the Rogue River) with a company of militia, a long list of grievances against the Indians, and a plan to exterminate them. After riling up the locals at a town hall meeting, and under the cover of darkness, Lupton and his company opened fire on a small Takelma village a short distance from the Table Rock Reservation, killing 23. All but four were old men, women, and children; they had been on their way to the Reservation.[17]

The Takelma and Shasta peoples of the upper Rogue had had enough. Led by Tecumtum, known to the Americans as "Chief John," they grabbed their weapons and fled the Reservation, moving down the Rogue valley toward the shelter of the wilderness in the Siskiyou Mountains, killing any white people they found along the way.

The final Rogue River War had begun.

◊

Even as open warfare broke out on the upper Rogue, the Tututnis on the coast remained peaceful. The whites in the mining claims around the mouth of the river were worried that the Takelma would persuade the Tututnis to join the war and formed their own militia company for protection. When it seemed the local tribes weren't going to immediately join the uprising, the militia, known as the Gold Beach Guards, concentrated on keeping the radical upriver tribes from moving down river to threaten them. To this end, they built and manned a camp near the Big Bend of the Rogue to monitor the hostile Indians' movements.

Two days before Christmas, 1855, a company of militia from Jacksonville attacked a village near Little Butte Creek on the upper Rogue. Between 19-26 Indians were killed.[18]

Then, about the same time, a militia company of whites from Crescent City attacked the Tolowa yet again, this time at the village of Howenquot at the mouth of the Smith River, just south of the Oregon border. Seventy Tolowa men, women, and children were killed.[19]

Still, the peace held on the lower Rogue. The people of the Yashute villages on both sides of the river had abandoned their homes and moved to the Tututni village four miles upriver. The treaty of the previous September had ordered this gathering to facilitate the relocation to the Reservation on the North Coast. They had no way of knowing that the U.S. Senate had failed to ratify the Treaty and the Oregon Indian Agency was having trouble finding money to finance this move, so there they waited.[20]

In January 1856, two Gold Beach Guard members, Lt. John Clevinger and Sgt. Enoch Huntley, were ambushed and killed about fifteen miles upriver while on their way to the camp at Big Bend. One of their guides, a Canadian mixed-blood Indian named Enos, who had reportedly come to the west coast as a guide with John Fremont in 1846, returned to the settlement at the mouth of the Rogue to report the attack and request more powder and ammunition for the militia at the Big Bend. The miners readily provided the requested ammunition. Enos headed back upriver and promptly disappeared.[21]

The Gold Beach Guard, officially Company "K" of the 2nd Regiment of the Oregon Mounted Volunteers, now highly suspicious of their Tututni neighbors, brought their members back from the Big Bend and set up camp across the river from the Tututnis, on the old treaty grounds.[22]

For the Tututni, who were well aware of the attacks made by other vigilante groups on sleeping villages along the upper Rogue and in California, the positioning of the Gold Beach Guards directly across the river from their village meant they were in immediate danger. Runners were sent to all the other villages in the area.[23]

◊

It was still winter on the Oregon coast. The storms swept out of the southwest, drenching the valleys with rain and scouring the headlands with 80 mph winds. The wind drove the ocean swells into pounding breakers, making the river bars nearly impassable. The rivers and creeks ran high, muddy, and cold. Snow blanketed the higher mountains and ridges, making the overland trails nearly impassable. It would have been wet, cold, and miserable for any traveler. Most people did everything they could to remain under shelter and close to a warm fire.

Indian Sub-agent Benjamin Wright monitored the situation closely from his cabin in Ellensburg, urging the coastal tribes to resist the advances of the more militant Indians from upriver. As January turned into February and edged toward March, a tense peace held.

This was the situation on the evening of February 22, 1856, when the miners and handful of families living near the community of Ellensburg on the south side of the Rogue River gathered for an all-night dance at the Coburn & Warwick Hotel in honor of George Washington's birthday.

The dance was to be a rare chance for the miners to blow off some steam, a chance to forget the troubles of the day and kick up their heels. Fiddles would play; neighbors would sing and dance; good food and drink would be shared; gossip would fly. Children would laugh and play games.

A good time would be had by all.

Chapter Three

The Burning

The Death of Benjamin Wright, Indian Agent

In late February 1856, the primary task of Indian Sub-agent Benjamin Wright was to somehow convince the native peoples along the Rogue River to ignore the entreaties of the militant factions and angry young men and remain at peace with the white miners. One of the primary steps toward that end was the potential apprehension of the Canadian mixed-blood Indian named Enos.

Enos had facilitated, if not actually committed, the killings of John Clevinger and Enoch Huntley in January. More worrisome, he had disappeared with a supply of ammunition the Ellensburg community had thought was going to the militia at the Big Bend of the Rogue. It seemed, with good reason, that Enos had aligned himself with the

Takelma militants and was now traveling among the coastal tribes, urging them to rise up against the invading whites.

On Friday, February 22, 1856, Benjamin Wright had received a tip that Enos was currently hiding in the Mikonotunne village about ten miles up the river. The tipster told him that Enos was a "bad Indian" and the elders wanted the Agent to remove him from their village.[24]

Benjamin Wright was more than happy to oblige.

As darkness fell on that Friday evening, Benjamin Wright had made it four miles up the Rogue, to where the Gold Beach Guard was camped across the river from the Tututni village. After eating dinner with the remaining volunteers (a number had traveled downriver for the Washington's Birthday dance, leaving fourteen standing guard in the camp), he and the commander of the Guard, Capt. John Poland, walked a short way downriver to a cabin owned by Jerry Maguire to spend the night.

Sometime during early morning hours of the 23rd, members of the Gold Beach Guard heard voices and sounds that could have been a struggle coming from the direction of the cabin. But since they heard no gunshots, they were not terribly alarmed.[25]

What happened, according to Tututni sources, is that someone knocked on the cabin door with a pretext to lure Wright outside. When he opened the door, the Indian Agent was set upon by Indians with hatchets and knives. Captain Poland came to his defense, but both men were quickly overpowered and killed.

According to the same Tututni sources, Wright was scalped and his heart cut out of his body. His heart was then roasted and eaten by Enos and Chetco Jenny, the translator Wright had driven naked down the boardwalk of Port Orford.[26]

It seems Chetco Jenny had neither forgotten that episode nor forgiven it.

Benjamin Wright was dead and the war had come to the South Coast.

Attack on the Gold Beach Guard

Despite the commotion at Maguire's cabin earlier in the evening, the fourteen members of the Gold Beach Guard began the morning of Saturday, February 23rd as usual. Charles Foster, a corporal with The Guard, was sitting by the breakfast fire with his first cup of morning coffee. As he lifted the tin mug to his lips a bullet knocked it from his hands. He fell over backwards and scrambled into the brush as bullets and gunfire filled the air.[27]

The surprise was absolute. So was the victory. Within the first moments, nine of the fourteen volunteers in camp were killed. Charles Foster hid in the brush and hoped no one would notice him. Four others managed to do something similar. As far as anyone knows no Indians were killed in the battle. As the Tututnis celebrated their victory, the survivors hid and waited for the chance to escape.

The Death of the Geisels

Six miles north of the mouth of the Rogue River, lay the hamlet of Elizabethtown. This small collection of buildings served the miners between the mouth of the Rogue River and Euchre Creek a few miles to the north. A leading family in this community was John Geisel, his wife Christina, and their five children, three boys and two girls. Geisel and his wife ran a combination hotel/boarding house/mercantile store for the miners and occasional traveler. Elizabethtown, and the Geisels' establishment, sat where the trail from Port Orford turned inland along Edson Creek (following an

Indian trail), so Elizabethtown was a convenient stopping place for travelers.

The Geisels lived in a 30 foot by 35 foot two story house clad with whipsawed lumber, and divided into twelve rooms. In addition, they had three 14 foot by 20 foot one room mining cabins they rented out. Another 20 foot by 30 foot, single-story building served as a store.[28]

Contemporary accounts (admittedly slanted toward the white's point of view) describe John Geisel as always treating his Indian neighbors fairly and with respect. There is no evidence he was abusive in any way.[29]

On the night of Friday, February 22, the Geisels did not go to the community dance because one of their children was ill.[30]

Sometime early Saturday morning, the 23rd, the Geisels were awakened by frantic pounding on the door. Suspicious and still half-asleep, Mr. Geisel asked who it was. A Tututni woman who worked as a maid for the Geisels identified herself and said she had urgent news. As Mr. Geisel opened the door, a group of Tututni men pushed inside and quickly overpowered him. Christina Geisel was made to watch as they killed her husband and then, one-by-one, her three sons, all below the age of ten. The Tututnis set the house and outbuildings on fire and took Christina, her thirteen-year-old daughter, Mary, and infant daughter Anna with them as prisoners.[31]

Flight to Fort Miner

Michael Riley, Constable for Coos County (which included the entire south coast of Oregon at the time) was canoeing upriver with two companions early on the morning of Saturday, February 23rd to serve a summons. He was only part way to his destination when he and his companions heard sustained gunfire coming from upriver. His friends wanted to continue, but Riley convinced them to take him back to Ellensburg and drop him off first.[32] No one can know how many lives that decision may have saved.

Riley had been instrumental in building Miner's Fort on the north side of the river. When he'd returned to Ellensburg from San Francisco with his wife and child a few weeks earlier, he'd noticed that the miners had built two blockhouses for protection from Indian attack near the settlement on the south side of the river. While the idea was sound, to his consternation, the blockhouses were within easy rifle range of anyone in the forested bluff behind them.

Mr. Riley and D.S. Holton crossed the river and used oxen to pull driftwood logs off the beach and build a fort about a mile north of the Rogue. It was situated in a marshy field clear of trees, providing no cover for any attackers and a clear field of fire for anyone inside the fort. The ocean was to the fort's back, a hundred or so yards away.[33] It seemed a much more defendable location than the original blockhouses.

On that Saturday morning, February 23rd, Michael Riley ran into the Coburn & Warwick Hotel and interrupted the dance with the news that the Tututnis had attacked the Gold Beach Guard camp upriver. The response was immediate. While Riley left to wake his wife and child and shepherd them to safety, the men at the dance gathered their weapons and headed a short way upriver to slow the Indian attack.

The residents of Ellensburg grabbed every boat and canoe they could find and ferried themselves across the Rogue, then trekked the mile to the fort Michael Riley had constructed. Once there, men worked furiously to finish stacking earth onto the protective wall. They could be attacked at any time and knew it.

Finally, when everyone else had crossed the river, the skirmishers followed them. As they did so, the angry Tututnis fell on the deserted settlement of Ellensburg and set fire to every building, every sluice box and anything else that would burn.

As the surviving miners huddled in their fort and awaited the Indians' attack, they watched the smoke rising from across the river.

The Burning of Ellensburg

Within a day of the whites abandoning the community of Ellensburg, everything was reduced to a smoking ruin. And the destruction wasn't limited to Ellensburg or the Rogue River.

On Euchre Creek, ten miles to the north, Dr. White and Mr. Warner were spending the night at the cabin of J.C. Smith. Sometime Friday night, February 22nd, an Indian approached the men in the cabin and told them he had a nice otter pelt he wanted them to see. Mr. Warner decided to go take a look at it. As soon as he was away from the cabin, a group of Indians attacked him with hatchets.

Dr. White and J. C. Smith fled into the brush and driftwood along the creek and hid there while the Indians set fire to the cabin. Only after the attackers dispersed after daylight, did the two survivors sneak away and make their way to safety. Dr. White went south to Fort Miner and Mr. Smith north to Port Orford.[34]

Similar attacks occurred to the white settlements at Whaleshead Creek and along the Chetco River, where the cabin and ferry of A.F. Miller, who had massacred the Chetcos two years before, were among those torched. Virtually every cabin, corral, shanty, sluice box, and boat between Humbug Mountain in the north and Smith River in the south was burned.

As a military feat, the Tututni attack was brilliantly planned and executed. The Athabaskan-speaking Indians of the South Coast had attacked nearly simultaneously across the sixty-mile length of their country, caught their enemy completely by surprise, and overwhelmed them in a single day. Twenty-five to thirty-five whites—about twenty-five percent of the white population—lay dead among the ruins and the remainder hid behind the earthen walls of Fort Miner without any means of communicating with the outside world.

The natives of the south coast of Oregon had reconquered their homeland.

The Dead, a Partial List (February 22-23, 1859)
(Whites only, of course)

At the Maguire Cabin

Indian Sub-agent Benjamin Wright
Captain John Poland, Commander, Company "K,"
2nd Regiment, OR Mounted Volunteers

At the Volunteer Camp

Barney Castle, Sergeant   George McCluskey
J.H Braun   P. McCullough
E.W. Howe   S. Heidrick
Mr. Wagoner   Mr. Seaman
Henry Lawrence

Others

John Geisel   Mr. Smith
John Geisel, Jr.   Mr. Warner
Henry Geisel   Mr. Wilson
Andrew Geisel   John Jolles

Joseph Leroc
  Two Leroc sons
W.R. Tullus
Mr. Bossman

Martin Reed
  George Reed
Guy C. Holcomb
Lorenzo Warren[35]

Chapter Four

Under Siege

The Fort

The fortification the miners of Ellensburg used for refuge from the Tututnis wasn't pretty or impressive. It bore no resemblance to the frontier fort we know from Hollywood film: a rectangular stockade of ten-foot logs, each log carved to a point on top, with roofed bastions at the four corners. Instead, the walls of Fort Miner consisted of stacked sod and earth, creating a chest-high breastwork. Small circular bastions stood on the southeast and northwest corners. It was, in essence, a chest-high earthen berm, with the middle scooped out.

Miner's Fort formed a rough rectangle, 114 feet long and 68 feet wide, with an interior area of about 7800 square feet, a little larger than a basketball court. Within the stockade sat two windowless cabins built of logs chinked with clay. The larger cabin measured 49 feet long, by 48 feet wide. The smaller: 49 feet long, by 33 feet wide. Both cabins were scarcely five feet tall and had no chimneys, just a hole in the roof to allow smoke from cooking or heating fires to escape.[36]

The cabins, the only shelter from the stormy late February weather, were largely reserved for the women and children. Seven or eight white women were among those who took shelter in Fort Miner along with twelve children and four or five Indian mistresses of the miners. Social mores being what they were in 1856, the white women refused to share a shelter with the Indians, so they were given the larger of the two cabins and the Indian women the smaller one. The men largely made do outside.

Into this space were crammed about a hundred men, women, and children, trying to survive.

The Situation

The people in Miner's Fort were not prepared for a lengthy siege. The fortification had not been provided with a store of food, medical supplies, or ammunition. What food and ammunition they had were the supplies they'd grabbed and carried with them as they'd fled their homes.

The foremost issue on everyone's mind as they settled behind the walls of the Fort was the threat of an imminent attack by the Tututnis. They had good reason for this. As the extent of the destruction was fully understood, it became clear that the Tututnis intended to kill every white person they could find on the South Coast. Just because they had successfully burned Ellensburg did not mean they were either finished or satisfied.

According to survivor reports, on Monday, February 25th the Canadian Indian Enos was seen riding up and down the hills overlooking the fort on a white horse, haranguing his fighters and urging them to attack. They did, but they had to cross a lot of open ground and the defenders' fire overwhelmed the attackers. The charge fizzled out and the Tututnis retreated back to the hills. They never attempted to overrun Fort Miner again.

Most of the men in Fort Miner were armed. One did not attempt to build a life on the American frontier without some sort of firearm, both for self-defense and to supplement diets by hunting, though many may not have brought their weapons to the Washington's Birthday dance. According to one report, they had sixty guns in the fort, but most of the firearms were "fowling pieces" or shotguns, with only a handful of rifles.[37]

An archaeological excavation in July 2016 at the Miners Fort site found evidence of people melting down lead to cast musket balls, Minie balls and bullets.[38] In the early months of 1856, just about all the rifles on the Oregon coast would have been single shot muskets or rifled muskets. These were muzzle-loading weapons that required the user to pour a measured amount of gunpowder down the barrel, followed by some kind of fabric or paper wadding, followed by the lead projectile. A rod was used to pack the bullet and powder tight before firing.

Using one was slow and awkward by modern standards, but the more efficient breech loaders would not become common, even among the Army, until the American Civil War, four years later.[39]

While most of the firearms were muzzle-loaders, at least one of the bullets found at the site was the type used for a Sharps breech-loading rifle, the leading (and most expensive) firearms technology of the time.[40]

The archaeologists also found a notable amount of spent bullets in an area which indicates that they had been embedded in the west-facing walls of the cabins.[41] This suggests the Tututnis spent much of the siege sniping at the Fort from the only available cover—the driftwood piles along the beach. So, while the women were casting bullets, it is not unreasonable to think Tututni bullets were thudding into the walls of their shelter.

◊

Another concern for the refugees was their isolation. There were no telephones or telegraphs on the South Coast and no roads; they barely had a town. So as the survivors huddled behind the walls of Fort Miner, they had to wonder whether the outside world even knew about their situation.

The U.S. Army did have a presence in the area, but nowhere near enough to provide immediate help. Fort Orford, a day's march to the north, was garrisoned by about twenty soldiers. More than two days' travel south, Captain DeLancey Floyd-Jones commanded a company of the 4th Infantry Regiment at Crescent City, CA. A larger garrison was even farther south at Fort Humboldt, near present day Eureka, California.

Alerting any of these garrisons involved someone traveling for days through a difficult landscape now fully controlled by the Tututni. It was a daunting challenge.

Further away, two companies of dragoons were stationed at Fort Lane, near the Table Rock Reservation on the upper reaches of the Rogue, but they were already busy fighting the rebellious Takelma and Shasta on the east side of the mountains. There also was no direct route to travel from the coast to the eastern valleys.

Even farther away, to the north, was Fort Umpqua, (near present-day Elkton, Oregon) but again, no direct route from the South Coast existed. On the north bank of the Columbia River, across from Portland, stood Ft. Vancouver, the military headquarters for the Oregon Territory. If they were to help, Fort Vancouver would have to send troops by sea, probably by way of Fort Orford.

All this was purely academic for the refugees, since as far as they knew no one at any of these military installations knew they were in trouble and they had no reasonable way of getting word to them.

They had to assume they were on their own.

On Sunday, February 24th, the day after the initial attack, the men gathered in Fort Miner held elections for new officers for Company "K," 2nd Regiment of the Oregon Mounted Volunteers, otherwise known as the Gold Beach Guard. Not only had their ranks been decimated in the initial Tututni attack, but all the paperwork of the Company, including the muster roll, had been burned. Relf Bledsoe was elected the new Captain of the unit and nearly all the men in Fort Miner who weren't already members joined.[42]

The Gold Beach Guards organized shifts in Fort Miner, assuring that at least forty men were standing watch at any given time. They were not going to be caught unprepared again.

As a long shot, they raised an American flag on a pole above the structures of the fort, along with a white banner with the word "HELP" painted on it. They hoped a passing ship would see their plea and alert the authorities.[43]

That hope was about the only thing they had.

The Boat

Unknown to the people trying to survive in Fort Miner, word of their situation had already reached the outside world. On Monday, February 25th, as Enos led the unsuccessful assault on the Fort, an exhausted Charles Foster stumbled into the community of Port Orford bearing news of the attacks on the Rogue River. Charles Foster had been the member of the Gold Beach Guard who'd had his coffee cup shot out of his hand in the first attack. He had managed to crawl into some brush and hide until the victorious Tututni moved on. Thinking he was the only survivor, he had crossed the Rogue River and made his way overland, dodging hostile Tututnis, until he reached Port Orford two days later.[44]

The news had immediate effect. The citizens of Port Orford began fortifying their settlement and, fearing an immanent attack, refused to allow the twenty soldiers at Fort Orford to leave them to go to the Rogue area. It was a logical position. Twenty soldiers wouldn't have made much of a difference to the folks in Fort Miner in a military sense but would leave Port Orford defenseless.

Captain William Tichenor, the founder of Port Orford and driving force behind the settlement of the South Coast, set sail on his schooner, *Nelly*, heading south. When the winds wouldn't let him land at the Rogue, he continued south to Crescent City to organize a rescue.[45]

Back in Port Orford, a group of eight men decided they would not wait for help to come from outside. On February 27th, two days after Charles Foster arrived in town with news of the attack, they loaded ammunition and food into a whaleboat and rowed out of Port Orford. Somehow, they made it twenty-seven miles south to the mouth of the Rogue but found both banks held by hostile Tututnis. Rather than admit defeat and return to Port Orford, they decided to put ashore on the beach immediately behind Fort Miner.

Unfortunately, the late February surf was too rough for them and capsized the boat. Of the eight men on board, only two—Captain Davis and a Mr. DeFremery—were rescued and brought into the safety of Fort Miner. The other six: H.G. Gerow, John O'Brien, Sylvester Long, William Thompson, Richard Gay, and Felix McCue—were either drowned or killed by the Tututni sniping from the driftwood piles.[46]

The first rescue attempt had failed and now the Fort had two more mouths to feed. But now the refugees knew that someone was aware of their situation. Help would be coming. All they had to do was survive until it got there.

◊

Once it became clear that the Tututnis weren't going to immediately take the Miners Fort by assault, the refugees' attention turned from military security to other problems they had, such as how they were going to feed everyone.

A hundred people, more or less, were sheltered in Fort Miner. Twelve were children, seven or eight were white women, four to six were Indian mistresses of white miners, and the rest were adult men. If one needs 1000 calories per day to maintain a minimum level of health, (health authorities recommend no less than 1200 calories for women and 1500 calories for men), the people within Fort Miner needed to come up with about 100,000 calories of food every day. And that had to be achieved with only what they'd carried with them as they'd fled their homes. There were no nearby groceries or food stores. Whatever supplies the mercantile stores in Ellensburg may have had were destroyed when the Tututni looted and burned the buildings. Even if some supplies had survived, retrieving them would involve leaving the safety of the fort, traveling through land controlled by the enemy, and crossing the river twice, there and back.

What's more, it was the last week of February. Even on the relatively mild Oregon coast, it was winter, and most food plants don't produce in winter.

To provide some perspective, 100,000 calories would mean about 288 pounds of potatoes per day, or 100 pounds of dried beans, or 87 pounds of beef. That's per day, every day. It would be a challenge under the best of circumstances to feed that many people.

Archaeologists excavating the Miners Fort site in 2016 found cooked animal bones that had been broken into very small pieces.[47] This suggests the inhabitants were trying to extract every single nutrient from the food they had, probably by making soup. The people huddling in Fort Miner probably ate a lot of soup.

Archaeologists also found another clue to the food problem in Fort Miner. In the ruins of the smaller cabin within the stockade—the one the Indian women were occupying—they found the remains of a camas oven. This was a pit-cooking method the Tututnis used to roast the onion-like camas bulbs that grew wild in area meadows, perhaps right outside the Fort. Ironically, the Indian women were using Indian techniques to feed the whites while under siege by Indians.[48]

However, as the first week in Fort Miner drew to an end, the refugees knew that if they wished to survive until help could reach them, they were going to need more food.

The Potato Raid

On March 3rd, the decision was made to mount an excursion to secure some food. James Hunt (who had been wounded in the attack on the Guards' camp but, like Charles Foster, had escaped, in his case to Fort Miner) owned a barn the Tututni had not yet burned. Stored in that barn was a supply of potatoes he'd harvested the previous autumn. The barn was on the north bank of the river, about a mile away from the fort. All they would have to do was get to the barn, retrieve the potatoes, and carry them back.

Seven men volunteered for this mission, including the only documented black man in the area, "Negro Ned," who was in put charge of the oxen team pulling the wagon. As the barn lay at the bottom of a sloping hill, the plan was to leave the wagon at the top of the slope with a lookout.

The others would climb down the hill, fill bags with as many potatoes as they could, then carry the bags back up to the wagon and return to the fort.

The excursion went exactly as they'd planned. That is, it did until shots rang out, killing the lookout immediately. The other men quickly recognized an ambush and tried to escape. A running gun battle ensued as the men frantically scrambled back toward the fort and the Tututnis tried to shoot them down.

Only two of the seven men made it back to the fort alive. Killed were Henry Bullen, L.W. Oliver, Daniel Richardson, John Trickey, Adolf Smolt, and "Negro Ned."[49]

Once again, the Tututnis had defeated the miners. The white deaths now numbered well over forty.

History does not record whether they were able to secure any potatoes.

Ransoming Mrs. Geisel

During the first week of March, a miner named Charles Brown and his Tolowa mistress, "Betsey", began negotiating with the besieging Tututnis about a ransom for Mrs. Christina Geisel and her daughters, Mary and Anna. Apparently, Mr. Brown had always treated his Indian neighbors with respect, so they trusted him more than most white men. The fact that his mistress had kinship ties with many of the Tututnis and spoke their language was also probably of more importance than the histories of the time give credit.[50]

The Geisel women had been held by the Tututnis since the attacks of February 23, nearly two weeks before.

There is some dispute among sources about who initiated negotiations, but it is doubtful the refugees in Fort Miner would have known that the Geisel women were alive, much less prisoners. Add to that the miners' vulnerable position besieged in Fort Miner, and the likelihood of the miners approaching the Tututnis to try and ransom the Geisel women seems small. It also seems unlikely that any such entreaties from the miners would have been accepted by the Tututnis.

It seems much more likely the Tututnis approached the miners.

But why would the Tututnis do that when they were committed to killing or driving all the whites from their country anyway? At the beginning of March, the Tututnis had been quite successful; everything pointed to their ultimate success. So why begin these negotiations? Why seek a ransom for their captives?

Perhaps the Tututni captors were tired of feeding and sheltering the white women while getting nothing in return. Perhaps their idea in taking them had always been to use the women as bargaining chips, either in a prisoner exchange, or for goods. Perhaps they simply realized that these women were never going to accept a place in Tututni society and would always have to be treated as prisoners. We cannot know for certain.

Whatever the reasons, the Russian immigrant, Charles Brown, who barely spoke English, and his wife, "Betsey," a Tolowa who spoke the Tututni language, walked out of the fort under a white flag of truce. They were soon surrounded by Tututnis. "Betsey" talked to them in their language and soon arranged to exchange Mrs. Geisel and her daughters for two Tututni women in the Miners Fort, plus a number of blankets and a hat.

On March 6th, 1856, three days after five men had been killed trying to secure some potatoes from a nearby barn, Christina Geisel and her two daughters walked away from their Tututni captors and into Fort Miner.

In order to express gratitude to Charley Brown, a proclamation was drafted by the leaders of the people in Fort Miner paying tribute to "our fellow citizen Mr. Charley

Brown for his brave and gallant conduct."[51] No mention was made of "Betsey."

◊

As the second week of March 1856 began, the refugees in Fort Miner settled into a routine of avoiding the occasional shots the Tututnis sent over the wall and trying to scrape together enough food to keep everyone alive. The rain storms continued to roll in off the Pacific. In February and March on the Oregon coast, on average, it rains more days than it doesn't rain, sometimes in deluges. The temperature is seldom freezing, but regularly drops into the high thirties, so it would have been wet and chilly much of the time.

Did the men stuck on guard duty hang tarps to give themselves some shelter, or just endure the rain? How did they keep their gunpowder dry? Did they build fires at points around the fort to try and keep warm? Did they have to ration firewood, so they wouldn't run out? We don't know the answers to these questions. But it is not unreasonable to believe that for most of the men, and possibly everyone else, their clothes never truly dried out.

One hundred people crammed into a space the size of a basketball court with minimal shelter and almost no sanitation would also be an ideal breeding ground for disease. Think of the conditions in a modern refugee camp and the health issues that often develop. Miners Fort in March of 1856 was in most ways a refugee camp, with many of the problems common in such places and none of the modern conveniences like medicine and chemical toilets. How many of the refugees came down with respiratory infections? How many suffered from gastro-intestinal diseases? Influenza? Fungal infections? Cholera? How many of these diseases were made worse by inadequate nutrition? Inadequate sanitation? The general close quarters? The records don't mention anyone dying of disease, but sickness had to be a serious problem.

However they were still alive.

Thanks to the survivors of the capsized boat, the miners now knew that the outside world was aware of their situation and forces were being organized to come to their aid.

All the residents of Fort Miner had to do was survive until help arrived.

That's all they had to do.

Chapter Five

Counter Attack

As soon as word reached Port Orford of the Tututni attack on the south coast, Captain William Tichenor set sail on his schooner, *Nelly*, heading south to get help. As he passed the settlements he had done so much to publicize, the situation was heartbreaking. He recalled later: "All along the coast was nothing but a blaze; wherever there was a log hut it was in flames or in smoldering ruins."[52]

He had his ship drop him off in Crescent City to help guide the rescue force, then continue on to San Francisco and the headquarters of the U.S. Army's Pacific Region Command. In Crescent City, he urged the garrison commander, Captain DeLancey Floyd-Jones to march immediately to the Rogue, but Captain Floyd-Jones had only been in his post for a couple of months and refused to act without orders from his superiors. Captain Tichenor would have to wait.[53]

On March 6, 1856 seventy troops for Crescent City and forty for Fort Orford boarded a ship in San Francisco and steamed north. They were led by Captain Edward O.C. Ord. Another seventy-four soldiers commanded by Captain Christopher Augur left Fort Vancouver on the north bank of the Columbia River, headed for Port Orford.

The plan devised by General John E. Wool, Commander of the Pacific Region, was to launch a three-pronged attack against the hostile forces along the Rogue River. The California force, under the overall command of Lieutenant Colonel Buchanan, with Captain Ord and Captain Floyd-Jones, was to march up the coast from Crescent City, relieve the civilians at Fort Miner, then proceed up the Rogue River to the rendezvous at the mouth of the Illinois River. Captain Augur was to lead his forces overland from Fort Orford to the mouth of the Illinois River. The third prong was to be led by Captain Andrew Smith, out of Fort Lane, moving down the Rogue to the mouth of the Illinois. Theoretically, the hostile Indians would be crushed between the three columns as they met at the mouth of the Illinois River, near present-day Agness.[54]

While good in theory, General Wool, looking at a map in his office in San Francisco, didn't seem to be aware of the difficulties of travel along the southwest coast. Captain Augur and his troops arrived in Fort Orford on March 11 and almost immediately started toward the rendezvous. Captain Ord, and his troops didn't even arrive in Crescent City until March 13 and the expedition under Lt. Col. Buchanan didn't set off for the Rogue country until Saturday, the 15th. Without any way for the three commands to communicate with each other, there was no practical manner to coordinate the attack.

The plan was destined to be ineffective from the start.

The Battle of Pistol River

As the column of soldiers left Crescent City that Saturday morning, March 15th, the Regular Army troops had company. The citizens of Crescent City had raised a company of militia to assist the troops and provide replacements for the Gold Beach Guard which had suffered—presumably—serious casualties. Leading this group of thirty-four volunteers was George Abbott, the same man who led a group of volunteers from Randolph, Oregon Territory, in an attack on the sleeping Nasomah village at the mouth of the Coquille River, two years before. The Crescent City militia had been anxious to move against the Indians ever since Capt. Tichenor had arrived at Crescent City and were frustrated by what they saw as the leisurely pace of the U.S. Army.

The Crescent City column spent the night of the 15th on the north bank of the Smith River, and the next night on the north bank of the Chetco River, then remained in camp on the Chetco all day Monday, the 17th, drilling. At this point, Abbott and the Militia Company, impatient and undisciplined, decided to move on ahead of the Regular Army soldiers.[55]

By doing so, the Crescent City Militia marched headlong into a Tututni ambush at the mouth of the Pistol River. The militia lost one man killed and several wounded and ended up digging in behind piles of driftwood on the south side of the river as the Tututnis surrounded them. Many of their horses and supplies were lost.[56]

On Tuesday, the 18th, the Army column was marching north near Whaleshead Creek when they met two militia members who relayed the news that the Militia Company was pinned down by Indians and in danger of losing their horses.

In his journal, Captain Ord mentions the encounter with the two volunteers, then that they camped on the side of a mountain. It was a "pretty camp."[57] He doesn't seem terribly bothered by the troubles the Militia were having.

The next day—Wednesday the 19th—the Army column reached the Militia on the south bank of the Pistol River. As they approached, the besieging Tututnis retreated. In his journal, Captain Ord remarks that the Militia Company "has lost horses and one man – seem to have had a hard time."[58]

It appears that the leadership of the U.S. Army (as personified by Capt. Ord anyway) did not have much respect or concern for the Crescent City Militia. If the journal is a true reflection of the Captain's concerns, he spends much more time marveling at the scenery and the possibility of gold than on the well-being of the civilian soldiers. The disdain with which the Regular Army regarded the militia was common and well-documented through the Civil War. The Army seemed to regard the militia as more trouble than they were worth.

The Army, now with the Crescent City Militia in camp, spent the night of March 19th at the mouth of Pistol River. They had no further trouble with the Tututnis that night.

The following day, Thursday March 20th, Captain Ord's Army column marching up the beach reached the burnt-out ruins of Ellensburg. They exchanged a few shots with Tututni in the forested bluff above the south bank of the river but suffered only one minor casualty before the Tututnis retreated. The only serious injury comes that night when a corporal is shot by a nervous recruit on guard duty.[59]

Captain Tichenor spent most of the following day building a boat and by evening the force had crossed the river and established a camp on a bluff on the north bank of the Rogue.[60]

The siege of Fort Miner was officially lifted on Friday March 21, exactly four weeks after the initial Tututni attack.

Captain Augur's Offensive

While Captain Ord and the column from Crescent City camped near Whaleshead Creek and George Abbott's Crescent City Militia hid from the Tututni behind the driftwood piles at Pistol River, Captain Christopher Augur and his troops from Fort Orford descended into the valley of the Rogue from the high ridges they'd followed through the interior mountains. Captain Augur was performing his part of Gen. Wool's three-prong battle plan. It was March 18th, a full week after he'd arrived in Port Orford, and he expected to see signs of the other two columns, from the coast and upriver, but could see nothing. His force appeared to be the only American troops at the rendezvous.

Capt. Augur was nervous about hanging around too long. His force was relatively small and deep within hostile territory. After scouts could not locate either of the other two columns, Augur ordered his men to burn the abandoned Shastecoostee village on the north bank of the Rogue, opposite the mouth of the Illinois River (near where the modern town of Agness is located). As the plank dwellings and their contents began to burn, shots rang out.

Indians on the other side of the river were shooting at them. The soldiers returned fire. Two soldiers were injured before the Indians were driven off. With the village burned and two wounded, Capt. Augur felt his luck was running out and ordered his men to move down the Rogue Valley, hoping to meet Col. Buchanan's command somewhere along the way.[61]

◊

Colonel Buchanan's Command

While Capt. Augur's troops marched down the rugged Rogue River valley after destroying the Shastecootee village, Col Buchanan's command remained in their camp on the north bank of the Rogue River. They had relieved the survivors in Fort Miner and passed out food and medicine. The schooner *Gold Beach* arrived on the 22nd to transport the women and families to Port Orford, but there was a problem. Though the white women definitely wanted to go to the safety of Port Orford, they refused to board the same ship as the Indian women. The men who had lived with the Indian women wanted them to stay at the Rogue, but Col. Buchanan insisted that was not an option. All civilians needed to be evacuated.

For a while they were at an impasse, until the Colonel offered to marry the Indian women to their partners, which may not have even been legal (Capt. Ord thought not). That seemed to solve the problem. Two of the miners agreed (including the hero of the Geisel prisoner exchange, Charles Brown) and the evacuation of civilians moved forward.

Company "K" of the 2nd Regiment of the Oregon Mounted Volunteers, (The Gold Beach Guards) commanded now by Relf Bledsoe and supplemented by the volunteers from Crescent City, set up camp in the ruins of Ellensburg, across the river from the Army. Since the skirmishes of March 20, there had been no sign of the hostile Tututnis near the mouth of the river.

On Tuesday, March 25th, the schooner *Gold Beach* finally left the mouth of the Rogue for Port Orford with the married women and their families (including Michael Riley and his wife, Maria) on board. On the same day the Guards traveled up river to the big Tututni village four miles above the mouth. They found it deserted and burned it before returning to camp.[62] They encountered no resistance from the Tututnis.

On Wednesday, March the 26th, Capt. Ord was ordered to attack the Mikonotunne village ten miles upriver. When the soldiers descended from the ridge trail, they found the village of ten houses deserted and burned it. Almost at once, the Tututnis attacked from the timbered ridges behind the village. However, Capt. Ord had anticipated the attack and set a portion of his force in a strong defensive position. After a protracted battle, the soldiers succeeded in forcing the Indians away from their village and eventually across the river. Eight Indians were killed; one Army private and a Sergeant were seriously wounded.[63]

Most important, every major village on the lower thirty-five miles of the Rogue River had now been destroyed, along with most of the winter food stores. It had to have been devastating to the Tututnis.

The next month or so was remarkably uneventful. Capt. Ord and his troops spent time fishing, hunting elk, and building a trail overland from the Rogue to Fort Orford. The hostile Indians were keeping a low profile.

On the early morning of April 24th, a group of Gold Beach Guards set up an ambush at a large rock near the mouth of Lobster Creek ten miles up the Rogue. When three canoes full of Tututnis appeared moving downriver, the Guards opened fire. Some eleven Indians were killed, either in the gunfire or by drowning in the river while trying to flee.[64]

No Guards were injured in the battle.

The rock at the mouth of Lobster Creek is still known as Massacre Rock today.

Three days later, on April 27th, Capt. Ord was ordered to march south with his men to escort a pack train bringing supplies up from Crescent City. On Tuesday, the 29th, as his troops approached the mouth of the Chetco

River, they saw a group of about seventy Tututnis. At the approach of the soldiers, the Indians fled in two groups: one along the north bank and the second into the thick brush along the river bottom.

Ord's soldiers chased the first group of hostiles for about two miles upriver, then noticed the second group crossing the river behind them and fired a few volleys at the Indians, hitting a handful. With their quarry now out of reach, the soldiers returned to the river crossing near the mouth of the Chetco. There, a Sgt. Smith was mortally wounded in a hand-to-hand fight with a Tututni. The Tututni was killed. Sgt. Smith died in camp three days later, on Friday May 2.[65]

Cpt. Ord, his men, and the pack train returned to the mouth of the Rogue River without further incident. In fact, most of the patrols in the coastal region now saw little to no sign of Tututni activity. It seemed as though the hostile Indians had retreated from the lower Rogue completely.

The Tututnis' two-months-long reconquering of their homeland was over.

Chapter Six

Victory and Removal

By the time Capt. Ord and his company returned to their camp at the mouth of the Rogue River in the second week of May 1856, the war on the south coast of Oregon was all but over. The patrols mounted by the U.S. Army and the Gold Beach Guards moved with impunity up and down the river and across the rugged mountain trails. The hostile Tututnis had retreated into the wilderness of the Rogue canyon further to the east.

Should a group of whites happen upon a group of Indians, a few shots would be exchanged, but now the Indians were more interested in escape than confrontation. All the major villages along the lower thirty-five miles of the Rogue had been destroyed, along with the food the Tututnis had stored for the winter. Spring salmon did still swim in the river; elk and deer still roamed through the forested hills.

But the river was controlled by the whites now and the hills were in question. They could not harvest nearly enough food to feed their people without risking their lives at every turn.

By the middle of May 1856, the Tututni people had been reduced to much the same condition as the white refugees in Fort Miner had been in back in March.

In hindsight, it seems clear that the Tututni and their allies were destined to lose this war from the first shot. They were a loose coalition of about 2000 people fighting a nation-state of 32 million. And, like every other Indian nation that fought American expansion into their territory, they began with an economic disadvantage. The Tututnis were hunter-gatherers, foragers, who fed themselves by roaming their territory, harvesting food when and where they found it. As such, they had no dedicated military class. Every man who fought against the whites, was also responsible for putting meat on his peoples' tables. If they were fighting, they weren't hunting. If they were dead or wounded, they weren't fishing. The longer a conflict dragged on and the more casualties it generated, the greater the hunger grew among the people.

On the other side, the Americans could put an armed force into the field and keep them there for months with minimal economic impact. They could also absorb casualties with little trouble. The Americans would always win a war of attrition and fairly quickly.

Perhaps this was why the Tututni chose the surprise attack on February 23rd. They knew they couldn't win a prolonged conflict, so they hoped to win with a quick, brutal, and complete victory. Perhaps they hoped that if they killed everyone on the South Coast in one attack, the whites would decide to go somewhere else that was safer. Since no one seems to have asked the Tututnis at the time, we'll never know for sure what they were thinking when they attacked the miners on the South Coast. Maybe it was simply one last act of desperation before they lost everything.

Because they would lose everything.

On Tuesday, May 6, Captain Ord notes in his diary receiving a letter from Captain Smith reporting that some Tututni women had reported that the hostile tribes in the mountains would be open to peace talks. Apparently, the Colonel commanding the Militia on the upper Rogue sent the Indian women back with the message that "if the Indians wanted peace they must send in the head of Enos."[66]

Captain Ord writes that his commander, Colonel Buchanan, was enraged by the Militia commander's message. The following morning, Col. Buchanan sent his own messengers, in the form of two more Indian women, upriver to tell the hostile Indians that he would be happy to meet them and negotiate a peace.[67]

On Thursday, May 8 the military forces camped at the mouth of the Rogue River began marching east to meet the hostile Indians and arrange a peace. Captains Ord and Floyd-Jones, under the command of Col. Buchanan, moved up the south side of the river, while Captains Smith and Augur moved up the north side. Once again, they were to converge near the mouth of the Illinois River.[68]

A week later, on Thursday afternoon, May 15th, the forces under Col. Buchanan camped at Oak Flat, on the Illinois River, two miles above its mouth, and prepared to negotiate a peace. Between the 15th and the 20th, Colonel Buchanan met with a series of Tututni leaders. The Chiefs of the Euchre Creek, Chetco, and Pistol River bands, as well as the Yashutes from the mouth of the Rogue, quickly agreed to surrender. Two other Chiefs—Lympe, or "Limpy" and Cholcultah, known by the miners as "George"— Takelmas who had survived the flight from the upper Rogue valley did not want to leave their homeland, but were finally convinced it was the only way to guarantee the survival of their people.

On May 20, the Chiefs finally agreed to assemble their people and surrender to the U.S. Army at the meadows at the Big Bend of the Rogue in seven days.[69]

The Rogue River War appeared to be over.

But it was not going to be that simple.

The Battle of Big Bend

A week later, as agreed in the treaty negotiations, Captain Andrew Smith marched his soldiers up to the Big Bend of the Rogue to accept the Tututnis' surrender. It poured rain the entire day, drenching the soldiers and turning the mountain trails into muddy morasses. The conditions also delayed the arrival of many of the hostile parties. But at one point, Capt. Smith was assured that Chief "George" and his people were about six miles away. They were coming.

The Army officers were feeling confident that the war was truly about to end. During the peace discussions, it had become apparent that the Tututnis genuinely wanted peace. The conflict, and the Army's strategy of destroying the Indians' villages and food stores, had taken its toll. The Tututnis were exhausted, malnourished, and dressed in little more than rags. And both the Army and the Tututnis knew that the Indians would not receive terms nearly as favorable from the militias, should the militias find them first.

As the day progressed though, Capt. Smith began to sense that something was wrong. The Tututnis already gathered at Big Bend were no longer relaxed, relieved, and happy to be surrendering to the Army. Something had changed. They'd become surly, suspicious, and increasingly agitated. Capt. Smith didn't know the reason for this, but it made him uneasy.[70]

In hindsight, the reason for this change of mood among the Tututnis could be laid directly on the Jacksonville Militia. Reinforcements had arrived at their Camp Leland,

39 miles upriver from the Big Bend and the refreshed Militia decided to launch an offensive, rather than allow the treaty to take effect. They set up ambushes and shot the war-weary Tututnis as they travelled down the rapids toward the Big Bend or along the river banks.[71]

It was news of the ambushes upriver that had angered the Tututnis and Takelmas gathered at the Big Bend. Those who had been happy to surrender to the Army just a few hours before now began to suspect that the U.S. Army wasn't gathering them to accept their surrender, but to exterminate them.

The situation grew so tense, that Captain Smith decided to move his men to a ridge above the meadow and dig in for a fight. He ordered his men to avoid firing the first shot. His position was to be purely defensive. They weren't looking for a battle but would be ready if one was forced on them.[72]

At 11:00 the morning of Tuesday, May 27th, the Tututnis attacked. Only the steady fire of a mountain howitzer and a counter charge by Smith's men broke the assault. The Tututnis changed tactics and climbed the hills to either side of Smith's position to lay down a deadly crossfire on the soldiers. Captain Smith's men suffered so many casualties that they had to withdraw one of their flanks. The battle continued until almost midnight.

Smith had four men dead and fifteen wounded.

The attack began again with daylight on the morning of the 28th. Over the next twelve hours of battle, the Tututnis made several attempts to overrun the Army positions but were repulsed each time. Finally, that afternoon, Capt. Smith's exhausted, desperate soldiers heard the shouts and muskets of friendly fire. Captain Christopher Augur's troops had arrived on the battlefield.

Charles Foster, the survivor of the Tututni's attack on the Gold Beach Guard camp three months before and Smith's local guide, had crept out of the besieged position overnight and made his way downriver to Capt. Augur's camp, seeking reinforcements.

Augur's fresh troops drove the Tututnis back, off the ridges and ultimately to the bank of the river. There, with no way to escape, the Tututnis surrendered. No one knows how many casualties the Tututni suffered in the battle. The U.S. Army suffered a total of seven men killed and twenty wounded.[73]

The Battle of the Big Bend broke the organized Tututni and Takelma resistance. Even the most hardcore Chiefs now realized there was no point in fighting any longer. All that was left for the U.S. Army and the militias was mop-up operations against a few isolated hostiles still at large and the logistical challenge of moving the Tututni prisoners to a reservation.

The Battle of Painted Rock

A little more than a week after the battle at Big Bend, Captain Christopher Augur's company was moving down the north side of the Rogue River in search of holdout hostile Tututnis. On the morning of June 5th, he attacked a small village near Painted Rock, three miles downriver from the mouth of the Illinois. As the Tututni fled across to the south side of the river, they were immediately set upon by Captain Relf Bledsoe's Gold Beach Guard, who were waiting there for them. At least fifteen Tututni were killed, with more drowning as they were swept away by the river. Two of Bledsoe's Gold Beach Guards were accidentally shot by Augur's men across the river.[74]

This was the last pitched battle of the Rogue River War.

The Last Hostile Chief

On Sunday, June 29, 1856, Tecumtum, or Chief "John" as the whites called him, the last—and perhaps most fierce—of the hostile Chiefs led his people into Captain Edward Ord's camp on Reinhardt Creek, south of Humbug Mountain.[75] With his surrender, the war was officially over. Under Capt. Ord's protection, the last of the hostile Rogue tribes marched to Fort Orford, to join the other surrendered Tututnis.

On July 8th, some of the Tututnis and Takelmas were loaded onto the steamer *Columbia* at Port Orford and shipped north to the Coast Indian Reservation. The next day, July 9, the rest were forced, under military guard, to walk the nearly two hundred miles to the Reservation. The Indians who had once populated the banks of the rivers and streams of the South Coast were gone.

It had been about three years since gold was first discovered on the black sand beaches and the white men had begun to move in. Three years, for peace to be replaced by tension and conflict. Three years, and now the defeated, demoralized Tututni people were marched at gunpoint away from their homeland forever.

The white men were the sole masters of the land.

Chapter Seven

Aftermath

Trail of Tears

On July 9, 1856, about 125 men, women, and children of the Tututni, Takelma, and Shasta tribes left camp near Port Orford and began the long walk to the new reservation on the north coast of Oregon. A U.S. Army detachment of ninety soldiers under the command of Major Reynolds was assigned to escort them and ensure no one was able to escape.

On today's highway system, the journey from Port Orford to the mouth of the Salmon River measures about 161 miles. In 1856, however, there were no roads and no bridges over the many rivers. The actual journey the prisoners made was probably closer to two hundred miles.

Because there were no roads, no wagons accompanied them on their journey north. Instead, nearly

200 mules were brought along, with most of them serving as pack animals.

Most of the defeated Tututnis from the South Coast had already been transported to the reservation by steamer. These people though, considered the most hostile of all the combatants of the Rogue War, were to be punished by their white captors. They would be forced to walk.

The journey took nearly a month and no delay was tolerated. Stragglers were beaten by their Army overseers and any resistance or attempt at escape was met with deadly force. The column was not even allowed to pause to bury the dead.

There are no known statistics on how many died along the march to the northern reservation, but there is no doubt that many did.

The Death of Enos

As the Rogue River War came to an end one key figure was still missing. He was not mentioned in the accounts of any of the later battles, nor numbered among the dead. After the Battle at Big Bend, when the hostile Tututni, Shasta, and Takelma chiefs surrendered their people, he was not among the prisoners.

He was Enos, the Canadian mixed-blood Indian who had been seen leading the Tututnis in their attack on the refugees in Fort Miner. Mrs. Christina Geisel, during her captivity, had seen him among her captors, acting like a chief and treated like a chief by the Tututnis. It was believed by most miners and military leaders that Enos had not only organized and led the attacks of February 22-23, 1856 but was largely responsible for persuading the Tututni tribes to go to war in the first place.[76]

But now the war was over. Most of the Tututni had been transported by force to the Coast Reservation, or to the

Grande Ronde Reservation on the edge of the Willamette Valley. But Enos was not among the Tututni in either location. It was something of a mystery.

Granted, a few renegade Tututni still hid out in the rugged mountains of the interior. He could be there, hiding, lying low. If so, someone would stumble upon him sooner or later. Another possibility was that he snuck away from the area when it became clear that the Tututnis were going to lose the war. This seemed more likely. Rumors had him up in Washington Territory, hiding on one of the Indian Reservations there. But he could have gone anywhere.

A State-wide warrant for his arrest on murder charges was issued by the newly created Curry County.[77]

In late summer, 1856, the mystery came to an end when friendly Tututnis on the Grande Ronde Reservation approached Courtney Walker, the Indian sub-agent, with the news that Enos had just arrived at the Reservation and was hiding in one of the Tututni tents. Enos was arrested without incident and taken first to Fort Yamhill, then Fort Vancouver, chained hand and foot.[78]

In Spring of 1857, the newly appointed Curry County Sheriff, Michael Riley, took custody of Enos at Fort Vancouver and brought him back to Port Orford to stand trial. Unfortunately, the only witness against Enos was to be Christina Geisel and she could not be located when the trial began. With no witness, the State's case fell apart and the Justice had no choice but to order Enos released. Sheriff Riley escorted Enos to the local blacksmith to have his chains cut off. During this procedure, a group of armed miners, angry at the perceived miscarriage of justice, gathered around the blacksmith shop.

As soon as Enos stepped foot outside, the miners seized him, carried him down to Battle Rock and hung him.[79]

The miners had exacted their frontier justice.

The Last Massacre

For years after the majority of the Tututnis had been removed to the Reservation, a few stragglers still remained in the rugged hills. Some of them had avoided the initial roundup of their people; others, homesick, had snuck away from the Reservation and made their way back to the South Coast. For their own safety, according to the Government, the Tututnis could not stay there. They would be shot on sight by any miner that came upon them. That was the reasoning when the Oregon Territorial Government arranged to gather the remaining Tututnis and transport them to the Coast Reservation. The contract for this task was awarded to Captain William Tichenor, founder and promoter of Port Orford.

On June 16, 1858, a full two years after the official end of the war, Captain Tichenor, with security help from local volunteers, marched 150 Tututnis up the trail following Edson Creek north from the Rogue River. Most of these prisoners were women, children, and the elderly. Only nine were young men.

Still, Mrs. Christina Geisel claimed one of these men was among those who had killed her husband in the first attack two years before. She'd recognized him; she was absolutely sure of it.[80]

Capt. Tichenor camped his prisoners for the night near the ruins of the Geisel cabin. According to his report of the incident, the Tututni men were acting suspicious, like they were planning to escape. Nervous, he sent word to Ellensburg for more armed volunteers to help secure his prisoners. When the volunteer reinforcements arrived, they surrounded the Tututnis and as dawn approached, opened fire. Nineteen unarmed people were killed, including all the young men.[81]

The Geisels' had been avenged.

Capt. Tichenor gathered the surviving Tututnis and continued the march out of the area.

Now the war was truly over.

Now the Tututni were truly gone.

PHOTOS

The Geisel Family Cemetery, Geisel Monument

Miner's Fort Location

Tututni Village Location

Treaty Grounds/Volunteer Camp Location

Massacre Rock

Mouth of Illinois River/Rendezvous Site

Notes

[1] Wilkinson, Charles *The People Are Dancing Again,* University of Washington Press 2010, pg 58
[2] Beckham, Stephen Dow *Requiem For A People,* University of Oklahoma Press 1971, pg. 123
[3] www.ndndhistoryresearch.wordpress.com/20017/04/21/the-most-persistent-attempt-to-esterminate-the-tribes-beginning-with-the-yontocket-massacre1853/
[4] Beckham, op cit, pg. 135
[5] Beckham, *ibid,* pg. 137
[6] www.historynet.com/wright-might-among-oregon-indians/
[7] www.ndnhhistoryresearch.wordpress.com, *op cit*
[8] Parrish, J.L., *Report to the Superintendent,* 1854
[9] Frazer, Robert W., *Mansfield on the Condition of the Western Forts,* pg.
[10] *Crescent City Herald,* November 7, 1855, pg. 2
[11] www.historynet.com, *op cit*
[12] www.historynet.com, *ibid*
[13] Beckham, op cit, pg.
[14] www.history.net/wright.might.among.indians.htm

[15] *Crescent City Herald,* September 12, 1855, pg 2
[16] www.halcyon.com/FWDP/fwdp.html
[17] Beckham, op cit, pg. 152
[18] En.wikipedia.org/wiki/List_of_Indian_massacres
[19] www.ndnhistoryresearch.wordpress.com, *op cit*
[20] www.ndnhistoryresearch.wordpress.com/when-the-tribes-sold-everything-oregon-tribal-treaty-payments/
[21] *Crescent City Herald,* January 30, 1856, pg. 2
[22] Beckham, *op cit,* pg. 173
[23] Wilkinson, Charles, *The People Are Dancing Again*, University of Washington Press. 2010, page 125
[24] Beckham, *op cit,* pg. 175
[25] Beckham, *op cit,* pg. 175
[26] Beckham, *op cit,* pg. 176
[27] Beckham, *op cit,* pg. 176
[28] www.curryhistory.com/historic-resources/11-biography-geisel-family
[29] Beckham, *op cit,* pg. 177
[30] *Evening Star,* Washington, D.C., February 27, 1890, pg. 7
[31] Beckham, *op cit,* pg. 175
[32] Beckham, *ibid,* pg. 175
[33] Beckham, *ibid,* pg. 174
[34] *Daily Alta California,* San Francisco, March 20, 1856, pg. 2
[35] *Daily Alta California, ibid*, pg. 2
[36] Tveskov, Mark, Phd. *Lecture on Excavation at Miners Fort*
[37] Joseph Lane Papers, *Memorial to Joseph Lane,* November 5, 1856, R. Bledsoe, Captain, Co. K, 2nd Regiment, OMV
[38] Tveskov, *op cit*
[39] www.truewestmagazine.com/breech-loading-rifles/
[40] Tveskov, *op cit*
[41] Tveskov, *ibid*
[42] *Oregon State Archives, Yakima and Rogue River War, Document File B, Reel 2, Document 566.*
[43] Beckham, *op cit,* pg. 176
[44] Beckham, *ibid,* pg. 174
[45] Glisan, Dr. Rodney, *Journal of Army Life,* pg. 282-292
[46] *Oregon Weekly Times,* March 22, 1856, pg. 1
[47] Tveskov, *op cit*
[48] Tveskov, *op cit*
[49] Beckham, *op cit,* pg. 177
[50] Tveskov, *op cit*
[51] Curryhistory.com/historic-resources/11-biographies-geisel-family

[52] Beckham, op cit, pg. 177
[53] Beckham, *ibid*, pg. 178
[54] Beckham, *ibid*, pg. 178
[55] Ord, E.O.C., *Diary (in Curry County, Ore.),pg.*
[56] *Ibid,* pg.
[57] *Ibid,* pg.
[58] *Ibid,* pg.
[59] *Ibid,* pg.
[60] *Ibid,* pg.
[61] Beckham, *op cit,* pg. 181
[62] Ord, *op cit,* pg.
[63] *Ibid,* pg.
[64] Beckham, *op cit,* pg. 184
[65] Ord, *op cit,* pg.
[66] *Ibid,* pg.
[67] *Ibid,* pg.
[68] *Ibid,* pg.
[69] Beckham, *op cit.,* pg. 185
[70] *Ibid,* pg. 186
[71] *Ibid,* pg. 186
[72] *Ibid,* pg. 186
[73] *Ibid,* pg. 187
[74] Ord, *op cit,* pg
[75] *Ibid,* pg
[76] Beckham, *op cit.,* pg.
[77] Dodge, Orville, *Pioneer History of Coos and Curry County,* pg. 347
[78] *Ibid*
[79] Beckham, *op cit., pg. 188*
[80] *Ibid,* pg. 189
[81] *Ibid,* pg. 189

Made in the USA
Lexington, KY
02 March 2019